COLOUR ILLUSTRATIONS

Front Cover: By 1889, Watkin had extended the Met from London to the North-West as far as Chesham. Initially all services went through to London, without the need for passengers to change trains. This shows one of the first service trains (with an A class 4-4-0T No.4) in Chesham station waiting to return to London. These engines had been designed for use underground and thus had little protection for the crew against the wind, rain and snow of the Chilterns - especially so when running cab first. The uniforms of the Met station staff in front of the locomotive and the engine crew show a subtle difference in uniforms reflecting their respective grades. *(Ray East Coll.)*

Inside Front Cover & Facing: Each year the Met published *Metro-land,* a booklet publicising the attractions of their services. The 1924 edition included this map highlighting features of note. This one shows the Wembley Empire Exhibition and anticipates the new branch to Watford. *(CAF Coll.)*

Inside Rear Cover:
Top: The Met's long desire to have their Watford Station in the town centre is at last about to come to fruition with the completion of the plan to join the Met at Croxley Green to the nearby ex-LMS Branch, thus giving access to Watford High St. and Junction. However this involves the controversial closure of the existing Met Station, shown above with a new S8 stock train in the foreground. *(sparkyscrum)*

Bottom: Reflecting their origin, TfL and LUL enthusiastically celebrated in 2013 the 150th anniversary of the opening of the Metropolitan Railway with many events. For many, the highlight was the running of a restored vintage steam-hauled train master-minded by Andy Barr. It consisted of the Met E class engine No.1 hauling a milk van, Jubilee coach No.353 and the Chesham shuttle Ashbury coaches. This shows them later on the 16th July 2014 at Chorleywood, marking the 150th anniversary of the Chesham shuttle. *(N. Brodrick/RM)*

Rear Cover: This plaque containing both crests of the Met was mounted at Neasden Works recording the Chief Mechanical Engineers of the Met.

Other books by the Author about the Metropolitan Railway
> *Chesham Shuttle, 1996*
> *Chesham Branch Album, 1998*
> *The Story of the Met & GC Joint Line, 2000*
> *Memories of the Met & GC Joint Line, 2002*
> *Rails to Metro-land, 2005*
> *The Metropolitan Line – London's first underground railway, 2010*
> *Images of 150 years of the Metropolitan Railway, 2012*
> *Echoes of the 'Met' Line, 2014*

Abbreviations

A&BR	Aylesbury & Buckingham Railway
BCRO	Buckinghamshire County Record Office
CAF	Clive Foxell Collection
ELR	East London Railway
GCR	Great Central Railway
ILN	Illustrated London News
GWR	Great Western Railway
LCDR	London, Chatham & Dover Railway
LLRRO	Leicestershire, Leicester & Rutland Record Office
LMS	London Midland & Scottish Railway
LNER	London North Eastern Railway
LNWR	London North Western Railway
LPC	Locomotive Publishing Co.
LT	London Transport & all its manifestations i.e. LPTB, LUL etc.
LTM	©T/L from the London Transport Museum Collection
LURS	London Underground Railway Society
Met	Metropolitan Railway
MDR	Metropolitan District Railway
MS&LR	Manchester Sheffield & Lincoln Railway
ILN	Illustrated London News
RCTS	Railway Correspondence & Travel Society
SER	South Eastern Railway
T/L	Transport for London

To all those who built, worked and travelled on the 'Met'

FIRST PUBLISHED 2015

Published by Clive Foxell
at 4 Meades Lane, Chesham, Bucks. HP5 1ND
clive.foxell@btinternet.com
In association with JPS Stationers Ltd.
www.jpsstationers.co.uk

Copyright © 2015 Clive Foxell

All rights reserved. No part of this publication may be reproduced, stored in a retrieval system, or transmitted in any form or by any means electronic, mechanical, photocopying and recording or otherwise, without permission in writing by the author.

ISBN 978 0 9564178 4 8

Printed by: Orbitpress Ltd,
11 Market Square, Chesham,
Bucks, HP5 1HG

Opposite: From Met publicity for the opening of the electrified branch to Watford in 1925.

SHADOWS OF THE METROPOLITAN RAILWAY

- and its associated companies

DR CLIVE FOXELL CBE FREng

'Metro-land - lies mostly in parts of Middlesex, Herts & Bucks and covers as much of the countryside as may conveniently be reached on foot from one Metropolitan Railway Station to another. It is a country of hills and valleys, ridges and bottoms, with a few broad level plateaux, here too are prim little towns which keep their old-world aspect. Yet houses multiply and new townships arise.' (From various editions of the 'Metro-land books')

'Situated in the heart of the country, yet within easy reach of the Metropolis, is ideal for the home life. It is surrounded by open country, including the wide expanses of The Common, and many acres of sports grounds; an excellent Golf Course is adjacent and tennis courts are available on the Estate itself. The altitude is 280 feet; gas, electric light, and water services are laid on together with main drainage; whilst the subsoil is gravely. The City and West End are easily accessible' (Henry J. Clarke, Builder of 4-bedroom & garage detached houses for £1,075 in 1932)

CONTENTS

The First Underground Railway p11
The City of London Solicitor had been worried about its infrastructure due to congestion by horse transport and also farm animals being taken to markets. He proposed an underground railway but, due to financial and public concerns, it was not until 1863 that a line opened between Paddington and Farringdon. It was a great success, with people's fears of subterranean travel proving unfounded.

Watkin Takes Over p18
However, due to poor financial control, a new Chairman was appointed in 1872. He was Edward Watkin, a Manchester entrepreneur with political and international business interests, who was charismatic but forceful, litigious and prone to dubious financial methods. He already controlled railways in the north and south of England, as well as Chemin de Fer du Nord, and then used the Met as a pawn to link these railways to join Manchester and Paris. He surreptitiously extended the Met through Bucks so his MS&LR could run trains over it to London, where he built a new terminus at Marylebone in 1899. But his death ended his plan, leaving the Met to share its tracks with the MS&LR, now a competitor. Indeed this relationship became so acrimonious that they were forced to form an uneasy Joint Company.

Selbie and Metro-land p37
Fortunately the warring Managers of the two companies retired and in the 1900's were replaced by Sam Fay (now-GCR) and Robert Selbie (Met), who settled their differences in a more civilised manner. Selbie concentrated on upgrading the Met trains and introduced electrification, in parallel with increasing traffic, particularly along the loss-making Extension. He did this by developing housing on surplus land near the Met, with the objective of meeting the demand for aspirational, yet affordable housing, in the countryside - but within easy reach of London. This was marketed using a range of media under the evocative brand of *Metro-land*. So successful was this novel scheme, that by the end of the Met the profit from housing exceeded that of the railway.

London Transport Takes Over p73
In the 1920's political pressure rose to unify London's heterogeneous transport. The Met objected on the grounds they were virtually a mainline service, but Selbie's death in 1930 weakened their case and it was absorbed into LT in 1933. The Manager of LT, Frank Pick, sought to integrate all LT activities to give a uniform, seamless service presented in a positive, uplifting style. But the Met presented him with problems and he soon reduced their fleet of steam engines and loss-making services beyond Aylesbury. However, he had enough clout to start the quadrupling to Rickmansworth and electrification beyond. WW2 delayed these projects and the imposition of LT ways, so to many the Met seemed much the same.

Nationalisation v Privatisation p85
Nationalisation in 1948 brought LT and its Joint partner under British Railways, which eased their relations but imposed new standards, polices and controls. In following years political pressures with swings between Nationalisation and Privatisation plus financial turmoil meant that the Met Line tended to stagnate. However, after the disastrous semi-privatisation as Metronet, control passed to TfL under the Lord Mayor and significant revitalisation. The ageing A stock has been replaced by the new sub-surface S stock and a renewal of the outdated signalling systems is due. Nevertheless these and other changes to improve services inevitably mark further steps to eliminate the character of the original Metropolitan Railway from the *TfL* behemoth.

PREFACE

I owe an apology to the readers of my last book, where I stated that it would be my final one. However, fate acts in unpredictable ways and although my personal life has taken a turn for the worse, depending on my computer to access the outside world has the compensation that I have been able to continue my studies of the 'Met'. So here is yet another book illustrating the evolution of that fascinating railway, hopefully with some fresh images and facets of their activities.

It is salutary to reflect that the Metropolitan Railway existed for some 69 years and, albeit these were turbulent times under Watkin and Selbie, it established traditions and ethos that has influenced the subsequent 80 years within the changing forms of London Transport. However, as others have pointed out, gradually Frank Pick's desire for uniformity has almost been achieved, apart from the fundamentals of the routes involved. Whether these continue to be emasculated or the opportunities seized by the Croxley-Watford Link and the restoration of that between Oxford and Cambridge, remains to be seen.

My thanks to those who have helped me with the illustrations. In particular, John Alsop has generously allowed me to use some gems from his magnificent collection. Then as always, have the stalwarts, H.C. Casserley, Ray East, Stephen Gradidge, Richard Hardy, John Parnham and the London Transport Museum of T*f*L as well as fellow members of the LURS. The attribution of images becomes more difficult with the pervasiveness of the internet where such material is freely copied and so I apologise for any failures to acknowledge the correct provenance of any of the pictures.

I am also indebted to Brian Hardy and all those who suggested corrections to the draft, but any remaining errors are my responsibility.

I also feel that I must respond to the occasional comments on my works which complain about undue emphasis on the influence of the Joint and the lack of coverage of the inner London area. The first is deliberate, in that leverage of the dominant mainline partners both operationally and financially on the Extension has reflected heavily on the rest of the Met routes. With regard to the inner London area, there is a lack of pictures due to the preference of photographers for open air scenes and the past difficulties of photographing the darker underground locations. Nevertheless, I hope that the following images will remind readers of the long shadows cast by the Met.

Clive Foxell   2015

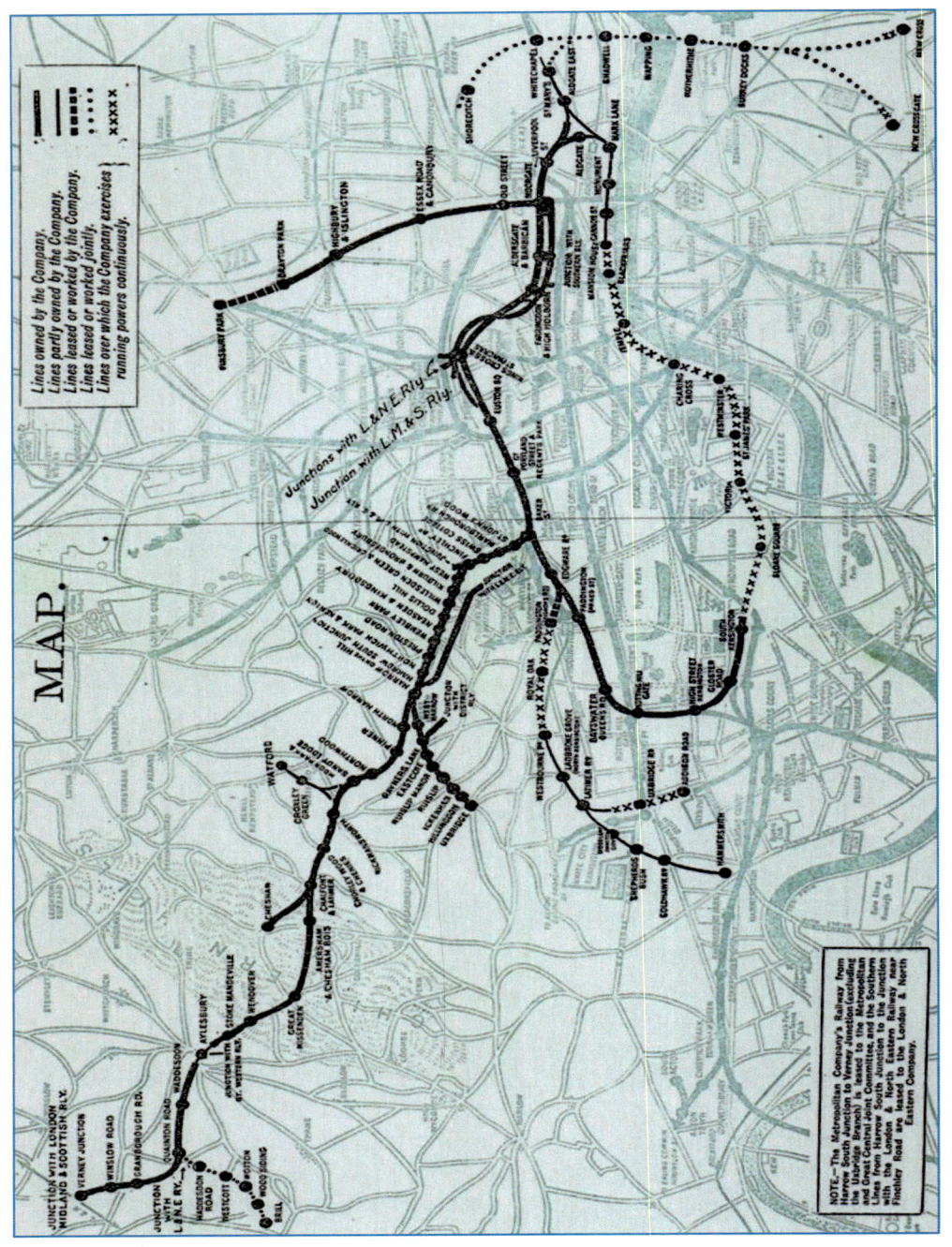

A map included with the Notice for the 1928 AGM 0f the Metropolitan railway. *(CAF Coll.)*

After long delay due to financial problems, in 1861 construction started on the underground Met railway from Paddington to Farringdon. The Chief Engineer was Sir John Fowler, but the tunnelling was undertaken by Sir Benjamin Baker. Most of the route was built by the 'cut & Cover' method, whereby a trench was excavated down the New Road (as above), covered by a brick-built arch and then the road re-laid over it. *(ILN)*

Looking eastwards, the Met station to be part of the Inner Circle is nearing completion at Paddington. This just has standard gauge tracks, but with some £175,000 the GWR had been one of the last to finance the original Met line from Praed Street, doing so to be able to have the advantage of running their trains through to The City. This involved the Met laying additional broad gauge rails. *(CAF Coll.)*

This Centenary parade attempts to recreate the formal inspection of the Met by VIP's before the public opening on 10th January 1863. However, in reality, the train had to be hauled by a contractors engine because the intended 'smokeless' locomotive by Fowler (and built by Robert Stephenson) was in practice a failure. *(Real Photos)*

King's Cross Station, in 1868, looking west. It was the largest Met station of the original line with an impressive overall roof. It had four tracks, the pair on the right being for GNR trains including a branch to their York Road suburban station. *(ILN)*

After the failure of Fowler's 'smokeless' engine the Met had to ask the GWR for help and so Gooch designed some 2-4-0T's with first condensing gear in the UK, to reduce emissions. They were the only GWR broad gauge engines with outside cylinders. This 'Metropolitan' Class, made by Vulcan Foundry, could run on the broad gauge tracks the Met had laid for the GWR trains and enabled the Met to start its services. *(LPC)*

However the GWR became unhappy over their share of use of the Met and in August 1863 they withdrew their trains, on which the Met depended. Fortunately, the GNR, also who wanted access to The City, helped out by providing trains. The engines were of Sturrock's Series 270, 0-4-2T's burning coke and with 'lashed-up' condensing gear. There were many derailments as one of the standard gauge rails had not previously been used. The GWR relented in October, but sold their Met shares. *(CAF Coll.)*

The opening of the Met encouraged the construction of an independent railway from Baker Street to Swiss Cottage in 1868, but as the area was then sparsely populated, it lost money and it effect was gradually absorbed by the Met. Marlborough Road was an intermediate station of this spur that was to feature in Watkin's future plans. *(Tony Harden Coll.)*

The entrance to the original Baker Street Station was just this small building with stairs to the platforms below. In front, the Met ran just under the Marylebone Road and it was easy to tell how the trains were moving as puffs of smoke came up through vents down the centre of the road! The later spur to Swiss Cottage is under Baker Street on the left, and was used by Watkin to launch his Extension to the North West. *(Tony Harden Coll.)*

The entrance to Portland Road (later Great Portland Street) Station was embellished to reflect that it was on the Crown Estate. Stairs led down to wooden platforms and soon ventilation ducts had to be added, and then fans. In 1866 the first of the Met fleet of buses started from here, running every 10 mins. to Oxford Circus. *(Tony Harden Coll.)* The picture below, although from a children's book, gives an impression of the atmosphere of the station

Jointly with the GWR, the Met extended westwards to Hammersmith in 1864. On this line Wood Lane Station opened in 1908 for visitors to the Franco-British Exhibition at the nearby 'Great White City' Exhibition Ground. The next popular event was the Japanese Exhibition of 1910, which inspired 'The Mikado'. *(Tony Harden Coll.)*

Opened initially as a temporary station in 1908, in later years the White City Stadium also hosted atheletics and greyhound racing which generated excellent traffic. *(LTM)*

In 1864 discussions began with the proposed MDR on completing an 'Inner Circle', but the financial problems of the MDR delayed progress. However to gain advantage, the Met started a Western extension to Kensington. This involved demolishing two houses in Leinster Gardens, but building false frontage 'to preserve the appearance of the terrace'. *(CAF Coll.)*

By 1868 the Met began services to South Kensington to join the MDR. Above is Notting Hill Gate station under construction in 1866 with staff and onlookers posing in front of the building, thought to be rather plain. There was much confusion with the nearby Notting Hill station (Hammersmith & City), which later became Ladbroke Grove. *(Henry Flather)*

Following their financial problems, Edward Watkin (a controversial Victorian entrepreneur) took control of the Met in 1872 and used it to further his wider ambitions for a Manchester-Paris railway. In his favourite smoking hat and Ulster he is visiting his South Eastern Railway at Folkestone to view progress on a new port and discuss his plans for a Channel Tunnel.

The East London Railway that had used Brunel's Thames Tunnel in 1869 for a line between Wapping and New Cross, got into financial difficulties, but when Watkin was appointed Chairman in 1878, he saw that by adding it to his Empire it would enable his trains from the North to travel from the Met, then via ELR and on to his SER- and so the Coast. *(CAF Coll.)*

After the success of the Met, there was a demand for the completing an 'Inner Circle 'and the Metropolitan District Railway undertook this. Although the Met supported this in principle, there were disagreements which were exacerbated by Watkin being appointed Chairman of the Met and John Staats Forbes to the MDR (as they were already enemies). Frustrated by MDR delays, Watkin extended the Met to Tower Hill, leading to more arguments until it was replaced by a Joint Mark Lane Station in 1884. *(The Guardian)*

Eventually the MDR completed its line under the Thames Embankment in 1884 thus facilitating the shared 'Inner Circle' services. To the East, the MDR built the Mansion House Station as a terminus, as seen above. *(nycsubway soc.)*

From the beginning, the links that the main line railways made with the Met generated so much traffic that the Met added more tracks - the so-called 'Widened Lines'. Looking down, to the west of Farringdon station, the GNR goods depot was on the left and the Met (Vine Street) on the right side. The Widened Lines came to carry much cross-London traffic. *(ILN)*

Just off the Widened Lines, the GWR built a goods depot under Smithfield Meat Market. With the trains in the background, this shows the lifts used to take the carcases up to the market floor. The basket from Aylesbury (probably of ducks) had come via Princes Risborough and Paddington. *(CAF Coll.)*

The early railways were primarily built to carry goods and passengers were secondary. As passenger traffic increased, they complained about the poor conditions and services the companies provided. However in 1844, Gladstone enabled an Act which forced the companies to provide at least one train/day which had reasonable steating and protection, travelling at more than 12mph and at a price of no more than 1penny/mile. These were known as parliamentary, or 'parly' trains, and this is such an Inner Circle ticket of 1898. *(CAF Coll.)*

In 1878 Watkin started steadily extending the spur to Swiss Cottage, on to Finchley Road, and then under the Rickmansworth Extension 1880 Act via Willesden and on to Harrow on the Hill in 1880. Here, apart from the historic connotations, there were the prospects of significant coal and other freight traffic and this started the first Met goods services. This shows the original signal box at the north western end of the station. *(LTM)*

This shows Northwood Station on the way to Rickmansworth. At this stage Watkin was trying to decide on the best route to extend the Met to join with his MS&LR to the North. Basically he sought a way, preferably by joining another railway's line (to save money), or pushing the Met through one of the gaps in the Chiltern Hills. *(John Alsop Coll.)*

Rickmansworth Station looking North West had been opened in 1887. The line had to be built on a sharp curve to avoid the nearby Rickmansworth Park Estate. From here, Watkin considered going on to High Wycombe, to Chesham (and joining the LNWR at Tring) or a new line through Amersham. *(John Alsop Coll.)*

Mainly because of his good relationship with the 3rd Duke of Buckingham, who was involved in the LNWR and the A&BR (and could facilitate a route to the North), Watkin choose to take the Met to Chesham. Work started in 1887 and this shows one of Firbank's (the contractor) trains removing chalk to create the line through 'The Backs' to Chesham Station. *(Ray East)*

Although Watkin had bought land from Chesham along The Vale to take the line on to Tring, his plans with the LNWR collapsed and so Chesham became the end of the Met line for a time. This shows a train about to return to London – cab first. The Railway Inspectorate disliked this and the Met had to install a turntable, just beyond the Signal Box. *(Ray East Coll.)*

For some time Watkin had his eye on the physically and financially frail A&BR, in that it offered another step to the North and so he acquired it in 1891. Watkin then decided to press on from Chalfont Road, to Amersham, along the Misbourne Valley and on to Aylesbury to join the A&BR in 1894. This shows the "first sod being cut" for this Met line at Stoke Road about ½ mile south of Aylesbury. The spade is now in the Aylesbury Museum. *(BCRO)*

Initially the Met started to build its own station at Walton Street in Aylesbury, but eventually it shared the existing station site operated by the GWR and A&BR. This shows a motley group of staff and onlookers at the first day of Met services from the new station in 1894. *(G. Aslett)*

The Duke of Buckingham was not only interested in railways, but also modernising his inheritance in Bucks and to this end in 1871 he built a light railway to transport materials over his estates, from Quainton Road (on the A&BR) to Brill. Originally dependent on horses, it later acquired steam locomotives which were prone to derailment. With the original Quainton Road station in the background (the Met later rebuilt it to the right), 0-6-0T *'Wotton'* is leaving for Brill over the track of un-sleepered bridge rail. *(Andrew Emmerson Coll.)*

The Brill Tramway harboured ambitions and had upgraded to some extent, however Watkin - who himself thought of using it to get to Oxford - managed to lease the railway in 1899, and soon started converting it to Met standards. This shows, soon after the acquisition, a Brill engine 0-6-0ST *'Brill No.1'* with a retired 8-wheel rigid Met coach. *(Mike Horne Coll.)*

Ferdinand de Rothschild chose to build his new Manor on the top of the hill at Waddesdon. In order to deliver the heavy materials, a connection was made to the Brill Tramway, 1½ miles away at Westcott and then Percheron mares hauled the wagons up the hill to the site. In 1877, this shows the construction under way, with the track in the foreground. *(Rothschild Archive)*

Around 1890, just north of Amersham, a cab-less 4-4-0T Met engine heads an up train of 8-wheeled coaches – some with the distinctive 1st class livery. Whilst on the right, a relatively new E Class 0-4-4T hauls a 'special' with the dedicated 6-wheel Rothschild saloons in the centre. *(John Alsop Collection)*

When the Met reached Aylesbury there was the need for replacement for the stalwart Beyer Peacock engines. To speed up matters, Watkin obtained the design of the proven Q Class engines of his SER and the Met ordered four from the same supplier. The resulting C class 0-4-4T is seen here at Neasden Depot *(E. Poteau Coll. No.22)*

Another of the four C Class 0-4-4T's, no.68 built by Neilson & Co. in 1891. Now in its final state with smokebox wingplates and condensing gear removed, plus a new cast iron chimney. It was sold in 1923 and finished life in a Welsh Colliery.

The A&BR between Aylesbury and Verney Junction had been opened in 1868 and, when it got into financial trouble, Watkin seized the opportunity to acquire it as another part of his scheme to link his Met and MS&LR. The Met had reached Aylesbury in 1892, but their existing engines were too heavy for the frail tracks of the A&BR and they had to loan some lighter GWR engines. So the Met obtained some 2-4-0T engines from Kerr-Stuart in 1894/5, designated Class D. But they had some problems and, as soon as the A&BR was upgraded, they were relegated to goods traffic – as seen here at Willesden Green. *(R. K. Blencowe Coll.)*

In 1920 Granborough Road (previously Grandborough Road) was typical of the Met-upgraded stations beyond Aylesbury. Looking north, by 1897 the A&BR light-rail track has been re-laid, line doubled and some 9 of the 11 level crossings removed. *(John Alsop Collection)*

After Granborough Road, the next station was Winslow Road, above, with one of the few level crossings left after the Met upgrade. Typically the use of 'Road' in the station name was a euphemism for in reality it was a long way from the place! It was situated in the area dominated by the Verney family, who later insisted on adding a siding for goods. *(CAF Coll.)*

At Verney Junction, Watkin contributed to a new joint station with the LNWR in the mistaken belief that this would become a major railway hub. It was built on part of the land owned by Sir Harry Verney who was a Met and an A&BR Director. Looking to Oxford, the LNWR tracks are on the right, with a Met train on the left. *(L&GRP)*

After many attempts to use other railways to link his MS&LR and Met lines, Watkin extended the MS&LR southwards to join the Met line at Quainton Road (above), However the antagonism between their respective Managers (who had been bitter rivals under Watkin) and which had already delayed construction, escalated into blatant obstruction. The ongoing animosity was to have serious effects in the future. *(LLRRO)*

In 1890, Watkin's Consultant Engineer Charles Liddell pointed out that Baker Street would not be able to cope with the extra MS&LR traffic and so a new terminus was proposed at Marylebone. This involved a tunnel under the hallowed Lord's Cricket Ground and Watkin had to 'buy them off'. A junction with the Met was made at Canfield Place and after more acrimony between the two Managers; eventually the first passenger train ran to Marylebone in 1898.

With the completion of the MS&LR London Extension, it became the Great Central Railway and the Manager's son (the enigmatic Harry Pollitt) designed the above Class 13 4-2-2's to haul the new expresses, seen here at Marylebone. But, problems at their Gorton Works led to Robinson taking over as Chief Engineer and producing an outstanding series of engines, such as the shapely 4-4-0 Class 11B No.1038, below *(CAF Coll.)*

Although GCR trains were now using the Met lines to Quainton Road, the old animosity between their Managers still existed, now made worse by the conflict between the GCR express traffic and the more numerous Met commuter trains. This was exacerbated by the contentious issue of apportioning revenues and led to the GCR forming a Joint company with the GWR to also run their trains via a new line from the Midlands. *(F. Moore's)*

Because of the growing goods traffic, two 0-6-0 saddle tanks were obtained from Peckett's in 1898/9. Near Neasden, No. 102 is hauling a train of spoil from the construction of the new MS&LR terminus at Marylebone. With the formation of the Met & GC Joint Ctte., these engines shared shunting on a 5-year cycle with the GCR and so were out of use for long periods. *(Peckett Ltd.)*

Separate tracks from Canfield Terrace for the GCR trains, parallel to those of the Met, were completed in 1901 and this shows another of the Robinson's well-propotioned 4-4-0 Class 11B's No. 1039 hauling a down train approaching Harrow on the Hill station, with the recently electrified Met tacks in the background. *(F. Moore's)*

The A & B Class Beyer Peacock locomotives, which had originally been obtained as an emergency action, became the stalwarts of the Met for over 40 years. However, their long use involving sharp bends and rapid accelerations took their toll on maintenance costs and as a result of numerous modifications, *'no two were the same'*. This shows Neasden staff posed in front of one of their charges. *(John Alsop Collection)*

The Class A/B engines were the mainstay of the Met for a long period, but due to their intensive use and stresses, particularly over the Inner Circle they were often in the shops for repair. This was not an easy task due to their construction and the Board of the Met frequently complained about the excessive backlog awaiting repair. *(H. C. Casserley)*

The first of the classic E Class 0-4-4T engines, No.77 was built at Neasden in March 1898 and was essentially an enlargement of the previous Stirling-type 'C' Class locomotives. This picture must date from after 1910 as the train form Aylesbury includes a new Pullman car. By this time the condensing apparatus had been removed from the engine. *(E. Pouteau)*

E Class No.80 was one of the batch of four engines built by Hawthorne, Leslie in 1900-1 at a cost of 70% more, Neasden being too busy. The down train to Aylesbury is near Wendover and just behind the locomotive are a Met milk van and a passenger brake van. *(John Alsop Collection)*

No.23 was the last of the Class A/B engines and was preserved: shown here prepared for the Centenary display. Their reputation was enhanced when an LNER pacific on a Leicester to Marylebone Express had broken down at Aylesbury in 1934. So Met No.23 (from its Brill duties) was coupled on and then took the 11 coach train over the Chilterns! *(R.. J. P. Mullett)*

With the spread of electrification, in 1905 the Met began to dispose of its stalwart Class A/B engines and Nos.13&15 were sold to the Cambrian Railway and duly converted to tender engines (Nos.34&36), to cope with the longer journeys involved. Above is No.36 at Llanidloes. Absorbed by the GWR as No.1113/4, they were soon scrapped. *(CAF Coll.)*

The consequences of the ongoing antagonism between the Managers of the Met and GCR came to a head when, on the 23rd December 1904, the 02.45 express from Marylebone derailed at the sharp S bend into Aylesbury, wrecking the station and was then hit by another train from the North. This is the scene with a Class 11b No.1040 in the foreground. *(R. Sedgwick Coll.)*

Clearing-up in the snowy weather after the disaster at Aylesbury Station. Looking north towards Quainton Road, one can see in the distance the GWR Goods Shed, built with its large doors to accommodate their wider Broad Gauge stock. *(John Alsop Collection)*

Confidential.

Metropolitan and Great Central Joint Committee.

MINUTES of MEETING of OFFICERS of the Great Central and Metropolitan Companies, held at 32, Westbourne Terrace, Paddington, on February 8th, 1906.

Sanctioned by Directors.
3rd May 1906 except
Minutes. 13. 19. 23. 40 & 41.

Present:

Confirmed by
Officers 20/6/06

On behalf of the Great Central Company.	On behalf of the Metropolitan Company.
Mr. R. HAIG BROWN,	Mr. H. B. PALMER,
„ C. T. SMITH,	„ W. H. BROWN,
„ W. CLOW,	„ J. H. FINLAYSON,
„ J. LEES,	„ F. CROCKER.
„ R. PASS,	
„ W. A. ROBINSON,	
„ H. M. BOWDEN,	
„ G. E. WARBURTON.	

1.—Joint Staff.

It was agreed to recommend, in view of the fact that the present staff on the Joint Line were all Metropolitan servants, it would, to enable the appointments to be equalised, be necessary for the Great Central to fill up whatever vacancies may occur until such time as the nominations in each grade by each Company are equal; subsequent appointments to be afterwards made alternately in grades by the two Companies; men nominated for positions as station-masters by either Company to be subject to the approval of the other.

The principle above referred to is that generally adopted in joint arrangements.

The Metropolitan representatives stated that at Aylesbury, the Station being joint with the Great Western, the above arrangements would not altogether apply.

The Aylesbury disaster was the culmination of the lack of cooperation between the Met and the GCR sharing the route into London, but fortunately the warring Managers both retired and in the 1900's were replaced respectively by Robert Selbie and Sam Fay. Although each continued 'to fight his corner', at least they did so in a civilised manner and this enabled their differences to be rationalised by the creation in 1906 of the Metropolitan & Great Central Joint Committee to run the shared tracks between Harrow and Verney Junction. This body split responsibilities for **all** the activities (from supplying buttons to appointing managers) on a 5 year cycle. Initially this resulted in some unworkable practices but these were to be modified by reality. The Minutes of the first Committee Meeting are shown above. *(CAF Coll.)*

Looking south over Aylesbury Station. As mentioned in their Minutes, this presented a problem to the new Joint Committee as it was already a Met & GWR Joint Station. So it now came under tripartite control, with management rotating 4 yearly. Thus decision making was inevitably slow, particularly improving the track layout after the 1904 disaster. *(CAF Coll.)*

In effect the 'Joint' was a separate company with its own staff, stations, signal boxes, purchasing of supplies such as tickets and uniforms, advertising and delivery vans as above – all with the Company name. Their accounts precisely apportioned the financial returns between the Met and the GCR, who carefully monitored financial expenditure to ensure it did not favour the other partner! *(CAF Coll.)*

In August 1909 the Chesham Shuttle was derailed near Hodd's Wood, due to a broken axle, causing disruption for some time. Probably the local paper, The Bucks Examiner, carried the headline *'London Cut-Off!'*. The engine had been one of the first of the B class engines which had larger coal bunkers and Adams bogies instead of the Bissell trucks. *(John Alsop Coll.)*

The next entirely Metropolitan designed engines appeared in 1901 and were built by the Yorkshire Engineering Co. The F Class were intended to cope with the growth in goods traffic on the Aylesbury line and were 0-6-2T's based on Clark's previous design for the E Class. They were the last locomotives to be built to the underground loading gauge. *(CAF Coll.)*

This is an F Class 0-6-2T running light on the up line, near Neasden around 1902. It is No.92 as it was the only one of the class that carried its number in small numerals on the side tanks. The date can be deduced as it soon lost its condensing gear after delivery from the Yorkshire Engine Co. in 1901. *(CAF Coll.)*

No.90 of the F Class was later fitted with Westinghouse brake; here the reservoir cylinder being on other side. By then the condensing apparatus had also been removed. The tripcock gear, for working over electrified lines, was fitted near the trailing pony truck. *(Real Photos)*

For many years the GWR and MDR launched schemes for lines to Uxbridge, but eventually local inertest encouraged the Met to operate a branch from Harrow in 1904. This shows building of the junction at Rayners Lane, with the Harrow tracks on the left and the controversial MDR connection to the right. Later sidings were added for a Met waste dump and for the vast amount of materials for Reid building Harrow Garden Village. *(John Alsop Coll.)*

Watkin and Forbes had reluctantly agreed on a common electrification system for the Inner Circle and so the Met extended electrification to the new Uxbridge branch. Looking towards Uxbridge this is Ruislip station, which had significant goods facilities. *(John Alsop Coll.)*

A closer view of Ruislip station; the major intermediate one on the Uxbridge branch. It was a focus for the intensive development of *Metro-land*, which also generated heavy traffic delivering building material etc. LT said that the population adjacent to the branch increased between 1931-9 from 48,300 to 100,600. *(John Alsop Coll.)*

Along the branch a number of popular 'Tea Gardens' were established, such as 'The Pavilion', offering peasant open space in the country for games, sports, picnics, dances and refreshments. These particularly attracted visitors from congested London, such as this party of children at Ruislip station. *(John Alsop Coll.)*

Initially much of the Uxbridge line was in open country and places like Ickenham were served by primitive facilities known as 'Haltes' (invented by the GWR). Ickenham station cost £275 and this shows it in the early LT days, still reflecting the modest Met station. Indeed, milk churns were still collected along the Uxbridge branch. *(John Alsop Coll.)*

The just completed substantial terminus of the branch at Belmont Road in Uxbridge. It was built on an alignment suitable for an extension to High Wycombe, where there was still dissatisfaction with the local GWR services. *(John Alsop Coll.)*

After the Met and MDR agreed a common electrification system for the Inner Circle, the Met ordered some 10 electric locomotives from Westinghouse to haul trains over the Extension lines. They were of 'camel-back' design with one set of controls in the centre, mounted on two powered bogies. However, the position of the driver restricted his visibility. *(John Alsop Coll.)*

Following their experiences with the first electric locomotives, the Met requirements were made more stringent and a new batch was obtained from British Thompson-Houston. Still a Bo-Bo arrangement, but with better acceleration (for the Inner Circle) and speed (for the Extension) and the body had controls at each end with a connecting gangway. *(John Alsop Coll.)*

The electrification programme involved the re-training of many of the operational Met Staff and this shows one of the in-house schemes. The staff called it *'moving on to the juice'*. (CAF Coll.)

The Great Northern & City Railway was a 3½ mile line from Moorgate to Finsbury Park and one of the first deep-level tunnels built to accommodate surface stock. The Met, under Robert Selbie, took it over for strategic, rather than revenue, reasons in 1913. This shows Finsbury Park with a GN&CR electric car set: these were rebuilt by the Met in 1915. *(CAF Coll.)*

Moorgate Station looking westwards around 1905. In completing the Met's part of the Inner Circle, Watkin obtained Parliamentary permission that land bought by the Met for railway construction, but was now surplus could be used for any other purposes. This gave the Met the unique right to develop such land – which led to *Metro-land*! *(John Alsop Collection)*

About the same time, this picture shows a Met C Class 0-4-4T No.69 waiting to depart from the bay platform of Baker Street (West) station with a passenger luggage van and train. To the left is the early signal box. *(R. H. Whitehorn)*

Watkin started his Extension towards the north-west in 1878 and the Met reached Willesden Green in 1879, but the extra tracks shown in this picture were not added in this section until 1915 due to the problems of widening the large bridges at nearby Kilburn. He negotiated interchange sidings here with the Midland Railway which enabled the Met to start goods services, in which coal became a major business. *(Tony Hadern)*

The Met had developed the Willesden Park Estate and by 1904 this had grown to some 3,000 houses and this led to much agitation for a convenient station. Eventually in 1909 the Met opened a new station with an island platform, named Dollis Hill & Gladstone Park. The above scene is looking westwards. *(John Alsop Collection)*

Watkin had been motivated to extend the Met to Kingsbury & Neasden after his friend the Duke of Buckingham promoted a new railway, the London & Aylesbury to run from Aylesbury (i.e. his A&BR) to his LNWR at Rickmansworth. This shows an A Class tank No.14 *'Dido'* leaving the station for Harrow. (*Brent Archive.*)

A closer view of Kingsbury & Neasden station. Originally just a hamlet, but it grew dramatically with the coming of the Met and Watkin's decision to move their engine depot from Edgware Road to Neasden, thus creating a Met 'village'. This was reinforced by him selling some adjacent land to the MS&LR for their London engine sheds. (*CAF Coll.*)

With the electrification reaching Harrow there was a lack of longer-distance multiple-electric stock and so the previously steam-hauled bogie coaches were converted with Westinghouse/BT-H equipments. This shows such a set with the windows for the driver in the coach ends, at Wembley Park station in 1924 - where the original two platforms for Park visitors had two more added with the quadrupling of 1914. *(John Alsop Collection)*

At Harrow on the Hill station in 1921, camel-back electric locomotive No.2 has taken over from the steam engine that has brought the train from Aylesbury, and will take it on to Liverpool Street. For operational convenience some changeovers took place at Wembley Park, but with the electrification in 1925 all would move to Rickmansworth *(John Gerchen Coll.)*

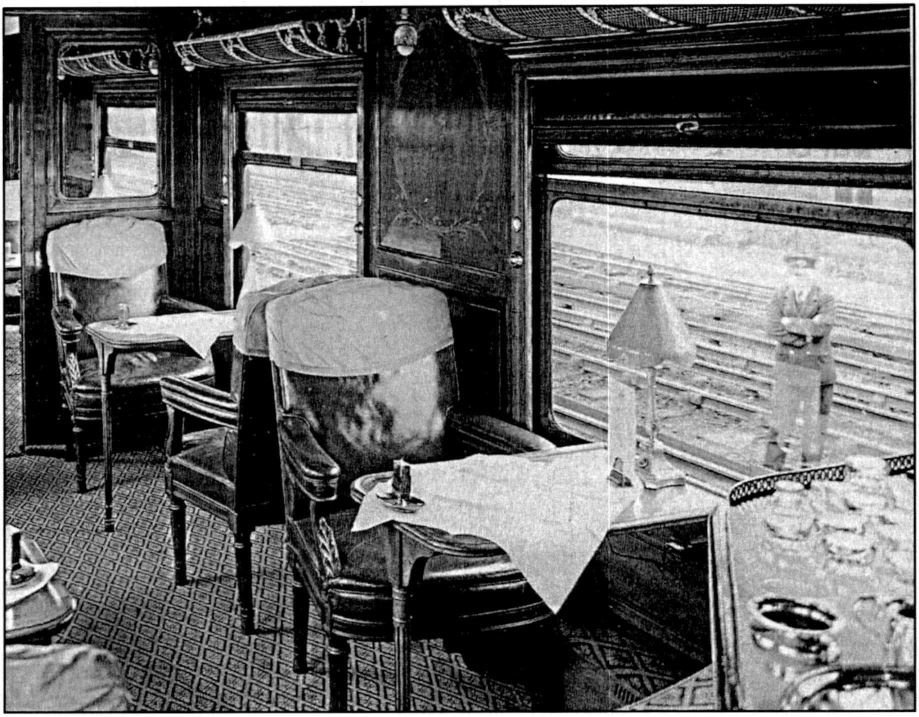

Like most railways the Met had experience of providing special coaches, in their case for the Rothschild's. So when the Rothschild's changed their allegiance to the GCR, Selbie upgraded the Rothschild's saloon and decided to match the other luxury GCR services with their own Met Pullman cars. So, in 1910 two such cars, named *Mayflower* and *Galatea* (named after yachts in the America Cup) entered service offering comfort, refreshments and toilets. Initially in Pullman Co. livery, this discoloured in the Inner Circle and in 1922 they re-appeared in Met crimson lake. The services between the City and Chesham, Aylesbury/Verney Junction were popular with businessmen, shoppers and theatre-goers. *(CAF Coll.)*

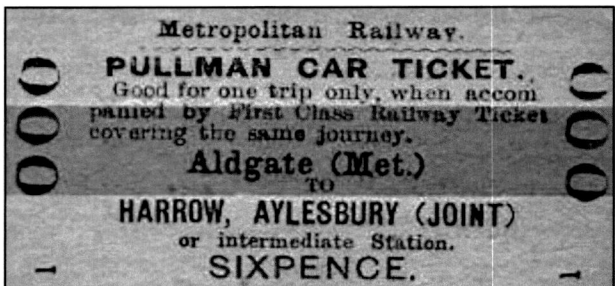

A sample ticket for the pleasure of travelling on the Pullman Car in an arm chair and having a G&T for 5p! LT considered re-introducing the service after WW2, but decided it was too much trouble. *(CAF Coll.)*

The parallel running of the Met and GCR trains symbolises the competition between the two quite different railways over the London hinterland. On the left, the Met camelback Bo-Bo No.6 is hauling a train with Pullman car to Harrow, where a steam engine will takeover to Aylesbury *(Gordon H. Tidey)*

A similar Aylesbury-bound train to that in the preceding picture, but now an E Class 0-4-4T No.78 has taken over at Harrow for the rest of the journey. It is probably about the same time, as the distinctive Pullman Car which carried this original livery from 1910 to 1922. *(John Alsop Collection)*

With the expected extension of electric set Uxbridge services to the City and their use on the ELR, the Met needed more trains. So, an order was placed with Metropolitan C&W for stock, which was delivered in 1913. This train has such end motor cars, with trailer cars of 1921. This later picture of 1934 shows a renovated train for the Circle Line *(CAF Coll.)*

Selbie recommended that four new higher capacity engines be ordered to handle more economically the growing heavier traffic and in 1915/6 the Yorkshire Engine Co. delivered the Class G 0-6-4T locomotives to the Met specification, but their design. This shows the first, No.94 named *'Lord Aberconway'* in the maker's photographic livery. *(Real Photos)*

A later view of No. 95 *'Robert H Selbie'*. No.96 which was named after its nominal designer *'Charles Jones'*, this was unusual as in other railways this would not happen until the Officer concerned had retired. *(John Gerchen Coll.)*

Here No. 96 is on an up train approaching Chorley Wood. When introduced, the new G Class engines were the Met's most powerful engines and were deployed on both goods and passenger trains. However with the subsequent delivery of the H Class 4-4-4T locomotives, the G Class were mainly used on freight trains, although there was a tendency to derail on the sharp curves in some yards, such as at Pinner. *(H. C. Casserley)*

Chalfont & Latimer station in 1919, with a down Aylesbury train headed by No.79, an E Class 0-4-4T. It had its coal bunker capacity increased by the addition of steel plates. Made by Hawthorn, Leslie it had just had a new boiler fitted from the Yorkshire Engine Co. To the far left, by the bay for the Chesham shuttle, is the site of the next picture. *(CAF Coll.)*

In 1915 Chalfont Road Station had become Chalfont & Latimer – Junction for Chesham, shown here with the proud Station Master George Ratcliffe. *(Agnes Barstow)*

The first major Met railway strike was in 1911 over conciliation procedures. The next was in 1919 caused by the Government withdrawing the wartime bonus payments to salaries. 15% of the Met staff continued to work and operated a skeleton service, as shown here at Northwood Station, where a Royal Air Force lorry is ferrying passengers. *(John Alsop Collection)*

The Met had employed few women, but with the outbreak of WW1 many of the male staff volunteered for the Services. So the Met started to recruit women for jobs ranging from cleaners to signalling. Above are a group of such guards at Neasden station. By the 1918 there were 543 women in total staff of 3,345. After the war, the men returned to those jobs. *(LTM)*

Work had begun to improve the design of the ageing Jubilee carriages to respond to the completion from the GCR on the Joint line. However, it was later realised that a radical improvement was necessary and this led from 1910-23 to the Dreadnought's from Metropolitan C&W which were longer, wider and more sumptuous. Above is a restored 1st class seven compartment version, whilst below right is a rear view of a brake 3rd showing the pick-up at the rear to enable the train (when hauled by an electric loco) to help bridge the breaks in electric sections. On the right, the luxury of the 1st class 5-aside accommodation can be seen. *(VCT; CAF Coll.)*

Winter conditions made the route over the Chiltern Hills even more difficult. On both sides of the Chilterns, at Aylesbury and Rickmansworth, it involved emerging from severe speed restrictions and having to climb to a altitude of 495ft at a gradient of about 1:100. This shows E Class No.81 with an up train in such bleak weather. At some places the Met installed line side fences to reduce drifting snow blocking the tracks. *(John Alsop Collection)*

As electrifiction spread and Selbie's new locomotives were intrduced, the E Class engines were relegated to secondary duties such as hauling the Chesham shuttle. However this was welcomed by the locals, for as is shown here in conjuction wiith the improved comfort of the Dreadnought coaches, it met the long standing complaints about the previous venerable trains. *(John Alsop Collection)*

Looking south towards Finchley Road, with the LNER tracks in the foreground and the extensive Finchley Road good sidings in the background. The down multiple electric Met train, consisting of a leading 1905 driving trailer, 1921 trailer, 1904 trailer and 1913 motor car. *(John Alsop Collection)*

From a similar position near Willesden Green, showing in the distance (top right) the Met sub-station at Finchley Road. The four car train of electric MW Stock is bound for Rickmansworth. *(John Alsop Collection)*

The Met G Class engines were intended for goods traffic, but they were pressed into service on the longer distance passenger trains. So to meet this need, a new design was produced, using some previous components, such as the G Class boiler, but with a more flexible wheel arrangement. Here No.107 of the resulting H Class 4-4-4T, just delivered from Kerr Stuart in 1921, shows it was probably the most elegant of Met locomotives. *(Real Photos)*

Inevitably, as the H Class engines were free-running and fast, they could be susceptible to slipping on curving gradients, such as here leaving Rickmansworth. However they could cope with the sharp bends on the Chesham Branch line. *(Real Photos)*

H Class No.106 at Aylesbury station with a train from Verney Junction. The tripcock can be seen between the wheels of the leading bogie wheels. The H Class were also fitted with footsteps on the front and rear buffer beam, as well as handrails to assist the enginemen on to the running plate. *(CAF Coll.)*

After much argument about the costs, No. 110 the last of the H Class was delivered in 1921. They had a fine turn of speed and sometimes carried the express headcode. Indeed, the RCTS recorded that on one occasion the 9.45 Aylesbury to Baker Street train attained a speed of 75 mph down Chorley Wood bank. *(CAF Coll.)*

Before long the H Class engines dominated the services beyond Harrow and here No.106 heads a set of six Dreadnought coaches near Wendover Dean. Expediency sometimes meant that they were pressed into service on goods trains, but the braking stresses caused severe overheating. *(John Alsop Collection)*

Meanwhile, of the five remaining Class A/B locomotives, two were allocated to the Brill branch – rotating on a weekly basis. This shows No.41 in the bay platform at Quainton Road waiting to return to Brill. *(CAF Coll.)*

As the number of railways grew, traffic had to pass over other company's territory to reach the desired destination. To solve the arguments over apportioning charges, in 1842 The Railway Clearing House was created to independently allocate the receipts from tickets; waybills etc., and as traffic grew this became a vast clerical activity analysing all the relevant paperwork. The picture below shows some of the hundreds of clerks at the RCH HQ near Euston, sorting out the myriad of tickets. The RCH also tackled the problems of ensuring all rolling stock could work together by creating standards. Also the RCH became valued as a neutral body where the different companies could discuss mutual problems and improvements. *(CAF Coll.)*

Many railways dedicated an engine in remembrance of staff lost in WW1. The GCR Robinson Class 9P No.1165 was named *'Valour'* and is seen here in the early 1920's with a down express near Wembley. Remembrance Day is still marked at Marylebone, often with the Type 66 Diesel engine also named *'Valour'* in attendance. *(Railway Photos Liverpool.)*

Similarly the Directors and Staff of the Met funded a memorial to those colleagues who had given their lives in WW1 and (designed by their Met architect Charles Clark) this was erected adjacent to platform 5 on Baker Street Station in 1920. It was recently refurbished and tributes are still made on the anniversary of The Armistice. *(CAF Coll. & Unknown)*

The Midland Railway had running rights over the Met's Widened Lines for some passenger services and also to access their goods depot at Whitecross St. Here looking east at Aldersgate station (now Barbican) a MR 0-4-4T engine fitted with condensing gear is at the right, whilst a MDR Circle Line train is arriving at the other platform. *(John Alsop Collection)*

In 1923 the majority of UK railways, but not the Met, were merged into four Groups and the GCR became part of the London North Eastern Railway- giving the Met's Joint partner more clout. Here a local train from Marylebone near Wembley, headed by an ex-GCR Robinson 4-6-2T, now Class A5 No.154 carrying an interim logo of L&NER. *(Railway Photos Liverpool)*

A picture epitomising *Metro-land*. He has just waved goodbye to his wife on leaving his £600 house at Chorleywood, set in the idyllic Bucks countryside. On arriving at the Met station he joins his neighbours on the platform where he knows his usual carriage will stop, puts his umbrella on the rack, sits in his expected seat and reads his paper until he arrives in The City - about an hour later. *(CAF Coll.)*

The scene outside Aylesbury station around 1920, with the forecourt filled with motor cars. The surplus vans from WW1 were already taking a significant amount of goods transport from the Met and, ironically with the growth of *Metro-land*, the affluent were acquiring cars – a trend which was to have a major impact on the railways, until eventually their vast number began to reduce the convenience of motoring. (BCRO)

Probably the one of the most significant of the Met's inheritances from Watkin was his acquisition of Wembley Park. In the 1920's they sold part to house the 1924 Empire Exhibition which generated more traffic, and continued to do so from the New Stadium. The rest of the land became the hub for major *Metro-land* housing. Above in 1922, the Stadium is under construction with the 4 craters where Watkin's Tower had once stood. At the top lies the Met line through Wembley Park Station. *(Brent Archives/Wembley History Society)*

Another major Met project at this time was the redevelopment of the Baker Street Station site. This shows the view from platform 1 of the demolition of the surrounding buildings and the construction of the siding that was to serve the flats and other facilities of Chiltern Court, by allowing goods to be delivered and rubbish removed by rail. *(John Gerchen Coll.)*

The creation of an appropriate headquarters at Baker Street was part of Selbie's desire to establish the standing of the Met and *Metro-land*. Work started in the early 1920's on an impressive entrance with a *porte-cochere*. Then in 1925, it was decided to add a building containing with the appropriate station facilities plus shops, large restaurant, dance hall and cinema. Above were to be superior flats, attractive to travellers using the Met – all this giving good returns to the Met. So Chiltern Court was completed in 1929 and this shows the side facing the Marylebone Road with the remains of the original entrance to Baker Street station in the foreground. *(Alan A. Jackson)*

The Met Architect, Charles Clark, also designed a new Headquarters for the Met, adjoining in Allsop Place nearby. It was in the same Edwardian style suggesting stolidity and reliability, but the main indication of a railway connection is the use of several full-size wagon drawbars to decorate the pediment of the facade. The building is still the location for the management of the Met Line and the rear overlooks the Baker Street West platforms. *(A Cabbies London)*

After WW1 the rise in goods traffic from the interchange sidings at Quainton Road, the limited number of G Class engines and the inability of the new H Class to handle the heavier loads led to the urgent need for more powerful locomotives. Ever frugal, the Met was able to obtain some surplus engines built at Woolwich Arsenal to the SECR 2-6-0 N Class design. And these were modified into 2-6-4T's by Woolwich and Armstrong Whitworth. Delivered in 1925, here one of the Class is at Quainton with the No.2 pick-up goods. *(CAF Coll.)*

The components used for the Met K Class engines came from a batch of 100 locomotives ordered by the Government to ensure retaining skilled staff at Woolwich Arsenal after WW1. These were to the Maunsell design at the SECR for an 2-6-0 N Class tender locomotive of 1923. Several railway companies bought these engines at a low price; which were nicknamed 'Woolworth's'! It is of interest that a preceding SECR locomotive of 1917 was the above 2-6-4 tank engine of the *'River'* Class. Many components of this were later used for their N Class engines, but because of their poor stability, the N Class incorporated many design features of Holcroft i.e. boiler and motion, who had recently joined the SECR from the GWR. So once again the Met had turned to the SECR for help with a locomotive, eventually leading, via Woolwich, to the Met K Class. As this photo shows, the similarities are striking, but Holcroft's modifications contributed to the pride of the Met. *(Horwich Photos)*

A Met down goods train breasts the Dutchlands summit, the highest point of their route over the Chilterns, headed by no.112 – one of the powerful K class 2-6-4T engines. The wagons are heading for the extensive exchange sidings at Quainton Road for onward destinations. *(John Alsop Collection)*

Around 1930 at Aylesbury Joint station, a Met K Class 2-6-4T No.113 pauses with an up goods train from Verney Junction. These locomotives were capable of hauling trains of up to 600 tons, but in practice the limiting factor was the length of some of the goods sidings. Weighing some 80 tons, the K Class were the heavist Met locomotives and two coupled together were sometimes used for consoldating new tracks and load testing bridges. *(H. C. Casserley)*

For a long time the Met had considered a branch to Watford and in 1910 Selbie decided to act in view of the possible LNWR competition. Although land was acquired, there was a 12 year delay in construction due WW1 and difficult negotiations with their reluctant Joint partner – now the LNER. Here is Watford station after completion in 1925, with extended goods facilities. At the top it shows the effect of the Met not being allowed to cross Cassiobury Park affected reaching their desired station in the High St. *(Britain from above)*

The electrified branch to Watford, via a triangular junction near Moor Park, opened in 1925. Both the Met, and initially the LNER, provided frequent services. This view is of the up-side and entrance of Rickmansworth station, whilst on the left the new bay platform, for a saloon car (that had been damaged) converted into a double-ended motor coach to operate a 'shuttle' service to Watford for a short while. *(CAF Coll.)*

At the intermediate station of Croxley Green, this notice in the Goods Yard reflects that the Watford branch was under the control of the Joint Committee of the Met and LNER (as a sub-committee of the original Joint Committee of the Met and GCR). In practice, the LNER, having paid half of the costs, were unhappy that the branch mainly benefited the Met. This was made worse when they had to withdraw their trains due to lack of demand. *(CAF Coll.)*

With the 1925 electrification, Rickmansworth became the change-over point between steam and electric traction on the Met. This 1957 scene shows how the BR engine hauling an up train form Aylesbury has uncoupled and run forward to cross over, so that the Bo-Bo electric ('Edmund Burke') can back onto the train and take it on to The City. All this in less than 4 mins, using methods that probably today would not be allowed by 'Health & Safety! *(J. Gerchen/ Colin Tait)*

Until it was absorbed by LT, the Met continued to honour Watkin's intentions by providing a good service to remote Verney Junction (albeit in spite of there being few passengers!). Here an H class tank No.107 is about to leave for the City with its Pullman car, whilst an LMS Webb radial 2-4-2T No.6704 arrives with a train for Banbury. *(H. C. Casserley)*

This rather innocuous image is included to recall watching trains from Chorleywood Common in the 1930's where there was a considerable amount of LNER and Met goods traffic to be seen. These trains were full of colour and variety for, apart from the various standard railway company stock, there were many private owners' wagons and vans carrying their various names and distinctive logos. All were built to RCH standards and were virtually mobile advertisement hoardings. They ranged from local coal merchants to petrol companies and some such as OXO, Colman's Mustard, Cadburys and Saxa Salt were memorable. *(CAF Coll.)*

With the 1930's', the pressure increased on the Met to be absorbed into the emerging London Transport conglomerate. But although they argued that they had main line operations, they lost their key advocate when Robert Selbie suddenly in 1930, and so were incorporated into LT in 1933. However, the Met had a 'last hurrah' by opening their new branch to Stanmore, seen here under construction, in the last days of 1932. *(Clive Foxell Coll.)*

The branch was opened on the 9th December 1932 with this special train passing through the Kingsbury cutting. It consisted of pristine MW stock, with the Rothschild Saloon and Met Pullman car for VIP's, which included the Labour Minister Mr Prybus and the Met Chairman Lord Aberconway. Soon the Met would be absorbed by LT, but *Metro-land* has already spread alongside the line. *(The Railway Magazine)*

At off-peak times the service over the Stanmore branch was provided by a 'shuttle' from Wembley Park, using damaged saloon stock that had been converted into double-ended compartment motor cars with a driver position at either end. Here in 1934, LT No.2769 ex-Met No.69 is seen trundling along leaving Stanmore station. *(Ken Nunn/LCGB)*

The shuttle arriving at Wembley Park station, which passengers complained involved a change of trains. In both the above photos it can be seen that some motor car style rear view mirrors have been fitted to assist the driver's vision. *(LPC)*

In 1935 LT persuaded the Government to launch a 'New Works Programme' to improve and extend London Transport in conjuction with the LNER and GWR. The Chairman of LT, Lord Ashfield convinced the Government of the financial merits and Frank Pick, was responsible for the implementation, and saw it as means of intergrating the system in a way that would uplift the users. For the Met he sought to reduce the congestion on the Extension by electrifying to Amersham and quadrupling tracks to Rickmansworth - as well as extending the Bakerloo line to Finchley Road. This shows the progress being made by 1938 at Finchley Road, where the Bakerloo line extension had begun to ease the Met congestion. *(stations uk)*

A further step to ease the traffic flow was to create a flyunder just north of Wembley Park for the Stanmore branch trains to pass beneath the Met main lines thus avoiding conflicting movements. Here ex-Met Bo-Bo electric locomotive No.1 *'John Lyon'* and train (of unusually 7 coaches) pass over a pre-1938 tube stock acticing as Stanmore shuttle train (before the Bakerloo line opened to Stanmore). After the outbreak of WW2 work continued for a shortwhile to finish some works but then the rest were 'mothballed' for 'the duration' *(Topical Press)*

In the early days of the absorption of the Met into LT, an unusual scene of the Brill branch line with a train apparently conveying passengers on the main line. The train is just entering Waddesdon station, and is believed to be the early morning through working to Aylesbury. The engine is No.23; one of the two Beyer Peacock's then relegated to Brill duties. *(H. C. Casserley)*

Here taking water at Aylesbury station is the same Met engine allocated to that engine shed for Brill duties. However, it is now in 1936 and it is one of the first in its fresh new LT logo, but retaining its Met numbering.. *(H. C. Casserley)*

After being absorbed into LT, Neasden Works were initially uncertain as to what livery to apply to their engines and the first two to emerge retained the Met livery and numbering but with 'MET' on their sides. In 1936, here is F Class No.91 with one of the twice daily coal trains from Harrow yard at Rayners Lane junction, about to reverse along the Joint line with the MDR, along Roxeth Viaduct and into the South Harrow Gasworks. *(P. Q. Treloar Coll.)*

Bo-Bo electric locomotives No 6 (*'William Penn'*) and No.1 (*'John Lyon'*) outside the new LT Neasden Depot, and in their wartime LT liveries. During WW2 these locomotives received a plain grey livery and their nameplates were removed. *(CAF Coll.)*

Goods traffic became important to the Met and as *Metro-land* grew, by 1930 it had doubled, with bulk materials being the main loads. However, livestock was also still a significant factor. Above is a typical cattle van, lime-washed to prevent infection, in Quainton Road – where the station staff would be expected to feed and water the animals until they were collected. There was a scale of chages for the extent of this service. *(CAF)*

Although rail coal traffic continued to incease until after WW2, motor transport had drastically reduced livestock by the late 1930's. On tlhe right is the cattle/horse pen adjacent to Chesham Station after the last cattle had been unloaded in the late 1940's, comprising a number of Charolais cows for the nearby Dungrove Farm, overlooking the station. *(CAF Coll.)*

Met stations also delt with the railway parcels, Royal Mail and daily newspapers – which came in the early morning by a Marylebone train for local distribution.

Until the late 1940's, milk was collected in churns from a number of station, such as Chorleywood, for the Express Dairy Depot at Willesden Green. Station staff had the knack of moving the churns by rolling them on their bottom rim. *(Topical Press)* Pre-war, the famous Bertram Mills Circus toured the UK using a special train. So it was quite an event when they returned to their winter headquaters near Chalfont and Latimer station. Astute station men charged 3d for local people to look at the train with its various animals - and even sold the resulting manure for 6d a bucket. *(CAF Coll.)*

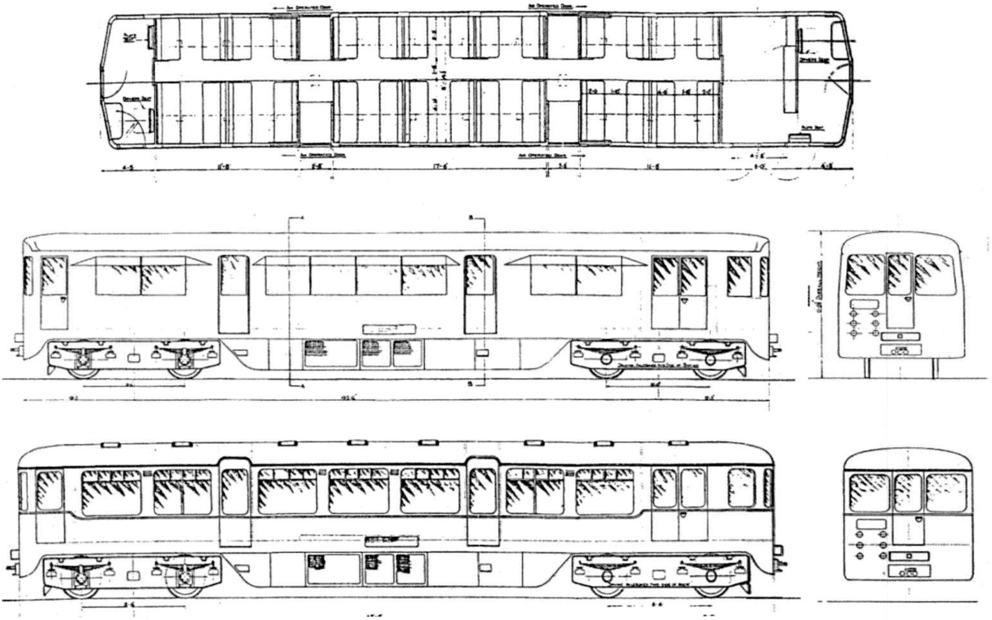

LT found it difficult to absorb the Met, who had well-established traditions and mainline pretensions, into its objective of an integrated transport system for London. In particular, the idiosyncratic branches in Bucks were questioned because of LT's desire to replace steam power and in the light of their intention to electrify to Amersham. Against this background, in March 1936 LT successfully trialled a GWR AEC diesel railcar over the Chesham Branch (also for possible use beyond Amersham). They then commissioned Gloucester Railway and Carriage & Wagon Co. to design a purpose-built railcar. The top drawing shows the resulting layout seating 50 with 3+2 seats and a luggage/parcels compartment. Two versions of the car (on the same diesel chassis) were considered. The middle diagram shows the influence of LT's Acton Design Office and the lower that of GRCW's – anticipating the look of future BR Dmu's. However this project was overtaken by WW2. *(A montage of material from N. Friswell/LURS)*

LT Acton Works then took over the design of the stock for the expected electrification to Amersham. To guide them several mock-ups were made (as above) and after the war this led to two experimental cars in order evaluate different configurations. These trials later resulted in the new A60 stock. *(Topical Press)*

In its new LT livery, K Class 4-6-2T No.112 is shown whilst shunting in Rickmansworth goods yard. The station man, with his shunter's pole (to handle the couplings without having to duck beneath the buffers) and flag, has posed for this picture by a visiting railway civil engineer. *(John Parnham)*

In 1935 an H Class No.103, also in the new LT livery, waits as it has done many times at Verney Junction, with a set of Dreadnought coaches for the signal to start on the journey to Baker Street. Although the staff were by now used to the lack of passengers, little did they think that LT would soon withdraw this service. *(H. C. Casserley)*

Frank Pick, the determined MD of LT, was concerned about the viability of the Met beyond Aylesbury and instituted a review in relation to the role of the LNER. This shows the special inspection train consisting of Dreadnought, Pullman & Rothschild salons hauled by Met H Class No.110, near Chorleywood in July 1935. It is unclear whether this train ventured over the Brill Branch, or the VIP's used the branch train! In any event, the fate of these services had already been sealed by their miniscule receipts. *(LTM)*

The above review was also influenced by Pick's successful launch of the LT 1935-40 New Works Programme which led to an agreement for the LNER (their partners in the Joint) taking responsibility for steam-working passenger services beyond Rickmansworth and Joint goods trains. Relevant Met engines would be transferred to the LNER, with the Met retaining some for engineering purposes. Here later in 1937 at the miniscule Rickmansworth coaling stage, newly painted ex-Met G Class No.96, has become LNER Class M2 No.6156. *(John Parnham)*

In 1938 the view from Roxborough Bridge, of the northern approach to Harrow on the Hill station. With the LT tracks on the left and the LNER ones to the right, this layout reflects the electrification of the Joint line in 1925. The layout was soon due to be modified, but this was delayed by the War until 1948. It was followed by a major track change for the 1961 quadrupling. *(Milepost 9½)*

In 1938, a grimy ex-Met K Class No.115 has breasted the Dutchlands summit with a train of goods wagons from the interchange yards at Quainton Road, bound for Neasden. *(Gordon Tidey)*

The transfer of the frontline Met Class G, H & K locomotives was part of the agreement for the LNER to take over the steam haulage of all Met passenger and goods trains. Here the Met K Class No.115 is waiting at the LNER Neasden Depot in September 1938, ready to go to Stratford for modifications and to emerge as LNER Class L2 No.6162. *(RCTS)*

In 1940 an ex-Met K class 4-6-2T – now in LNER Class L2 livery - comes into Amersham Station - with the up No.3 goods train from Verney Junction which is due back at Neasden just before Midnight having started out at 08.10. In the 1930's the Met had lengthened all relevant sidings to accommodate up to 40 wagons. (R. H. N. Hardy)

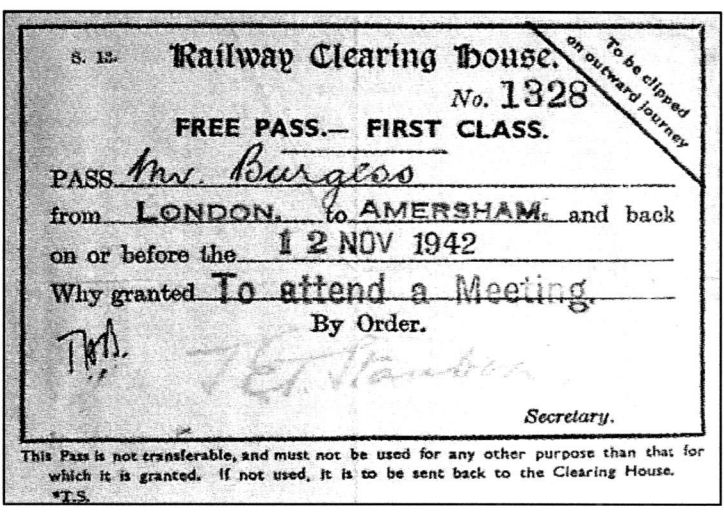

The RCH played a key role during WW2 and was evacuated from London, with part going to Coleshill near Amersham; hence the above Free Pass for use on the Met. After the War, in 1948 the RCH was absorbed into British Railways, although some legal aspects were not transferred until 1954. *(CAF Coll.)*

In London, the Met suffered badly from the effects of the Blitz, the later 'baby' Blitz and then the V weapons. This shows result of a combination of high explosive and incendiary bombs at .Moorgate on the 31st December 1940. The burnt-out train is of LT O&P stock. However the speed of recovery, depending mainly on manual labour, was remarkable *(Arthur Cross: Frank Tibbs)*

During and immediately after WW2 the Marylebone services relied to a large extent on the ex-GCR locomotives. Typical, is this LNER Class C4 4-4-2 No. 2948 with an down train of Gresley coaches having just passed Rickmansworth and beginning its ascent of the Chilterns. The grimy state of this once handsome engine in 1947 reflects the serious lack of wartime maintenance. *(H. C. Casserley)*

Another classic ex-GCR engine that continued through the war was from their Director D10 Class of 4-4-0's, now LNER No.5432 *'Sir Edmund Fraser'*, under repair at their Neasden Depot. Apart from the ongoing lack of maintenance due to lack of staff and investment, the Railway Companies were becoming inhibited by the threat of Nationalisation. *(CAF Coll.)*

In 1948 most of the UK's transport was nationalised under British Transport. Inevitably British Railways sought the 'economies of scale' by standardisation of the plethora of equipment and cultures. To this end, in June 1948 trials were undertaken of the various types of locomotive, with the mixed-traffic class being run over the Met & GC Joint line. Above, GWR Hall No.6990 *'Witherslack Hall'* arrives at Marylebone. However, the variety of coal, conditions and driving/firing methods rendered the tests inconclusive! *(CAF Coll.)*

With the nationalisation, LT also came under the BTC, which became mainly concerned with its relations with the relevant mainline Regions. In addition, the financial constraints limited the plans to upgrade stock and services. Thus the above veteran C stock set of 1910 continues to operate on the East London line at Rotherhithe. *(CAF Coll.)*

The LNER Class L3 2-6-4T No.9061 shunting at Aylesbury in 1948, yet to receive its BR livery logo. The state of the engine reminds me of when I was a casual Neasden cleaner at this time we were issued with paraffin and a handful of cotton waste and told to clean the motion beneath the running plate and the number – so the engine could be recognised! *(CAF Coll.)*

With the approach of WW2, the Chesham Shuttle operation had been simplified by replacing the E Class engine plus Dreadnought coaches by an auto train, so avoiding the need for the engine to run round the train at either end of the trip. However passengers were surprised to find it comprised a venerable ex-GCR Class 9K 4-4-2T engine with Victorian Ashbury coaches, as shown here at Chesham in 1948, with the new BR logo. *(CAF Coll.)*

An evocative picture of 1960 taken from the rear of the Chesham shuttle (an ex- GCR Class C13 and Ashbury coaches) as it leaves Chesham, entering an 'S' bend over two branches of the River Chess, before a climb of 1:60 up from the Chess Valley. The Met was only allowed to build these bridges if it *'did not interfere with the fish in the river'*! *(CAF Coll.)*

A 1958 picture of the Chesham shuttle, having arrived at its Chalfont & Latimer bay platform. The ex-GCR Class 13 4-4-2T now BR No.67461 is simmering whilst the passengers await their London train connection. Meanwhile the goods yard remains in use. *(Rodney Weaver)*

As the remaining Met steam engines began become increasingly difficult to maintain, LT initially considered replacing them with diesel-electric locomotives. But eventually from 1955 they acquired some redundant ex-GWR Class 57XX 0-6-0 pannier tank engines. This shows one of the 13 'red panniers' shunting a train of waste at the LT dump near the junction with the Watford branch. *(L. V. Reason)*

The new signal box with a 95 lever Westinghouse 'N' frame at Harrow-on the-Hill was not opened until 1948 due to WW2. This shows the track layout to the north, following recent changes. A new push button route-setting panel to Northwood was not fitted until 1962, after the major track quadrupiling works to the north. *(CAF Coll.)*

The Eastern Region of BR re-introduced named trains from Marylebone in 1948 and the earlier enlargement of the turntable at Marylebone, enabled these trains to be hauled by larger engines, such as Gresley's Class A3 4-6-2's. This shows his Class V2 2-6-2 No.60862 heading the down 'Master Cutler' near Chorley Wood Common, in 1956. *(L. V. Reason)*

In 1957 'The Master Cutler' has just past through Rickmansworth station at reduced speed (due to the sharp curve) and is accelerating past the goods shed. Headed by A3 Class 4-6-2 60059 'Tracery' and bound for Marylebone, the evening return run was via the GW&GC Joint line. The named services were to be withdrawn in 1958, following the transfer of the ex-GCR route to Midland Region control. *(L. V. Reason))*

Over the Widened Lines, looking East towards Farringdon Station. On the left had been the Met Vine St. Goods Depot and on the right that of the GNR. The train hauled by an E Class engine No.L46 is a Stephenson Locomotive Society rail tour, in November 1957, of the Inner Circle and here finishing the circuit by heading to Wembley Park via Baker Street. *(RCTS)*

The scene at Moorgate station in 1959, looking west where there is as yet little sign of the rebuilding of the bomb damage. On the right is a Met T stock train, whilst in the other bay platform a BR train is departing, leaving the engine that brought it simmering at the buffer stop. *(CAF Coll.)*

One of the early T stock multiple-electric trains originally intended for the City and Baker Street services to Watford and Rickmansworth (and in practice sometimes on the Uxbridge Line). The superstructure was largely of wood with decorative mouldings. Here in 1957, such a down train is approaching Rickmansworth. In the foreground the pre-war preparations for laying extra tracks have been cleared of under-growth, but the original plans for a 4-track station at Rickmansworth were to be abandoned. *(S. Gradidge)*

Again in 1957 at Rickmansworth, is one of the later variants of the Met T stocks', which were largely of steel construction, giving smoother exteriors. But by now the end was in sight for these stalwart Met T stock cars. Already the design work had started on their replacements and two T stock chassis's had been be used to evaluate possible design options. *(Tony Harden)*

The Joint Companies both benefitted from the events at Wembley Stadium, but the Met enhancement of Wembley Park station for the Empire Exhibition and experience dealing with crowds meant that they attracted most of the traffic. Indeed the LNER complained that *'you must not begrudge us any crumbs that fall from the rich man's table'*. This shows the fans arriving for a Cup Final. *(Daily Mail)*

Here a BR special is at the Neasden Junction for the Nottingham Forest v Luton Town Cup Final of 1959. Headed by a Thompson Class B1 4-6-0, with the now standard BR 'lion & wheel' logo on the side of the tender. *(Ben Brooksbank)*

After WW2, the 1935-40 New Works Programme to electrify the Met beyond Rickmansworth was re-started and this was the scene of the tracks being quadrupled. Looking north at Moor Park in 1960 and passing the preparations is an up semi-fast Woodford to Marylebone headed by a Class B1 4-6-0 No. 61186 based at Woodford Hulse. *(D. Trevor Rowe)*

The original tracks, down platform and bridge of the ramshackle Moor Park station are on the left and centre. The extra tracks and a new island platform for stopping trains are on the right and to the left a similar platform will also be built between far tracks for the fast Met and also BR Marylebone trains. *(Brooks Photos)*

On the 9th August 1959, the RCTS ran a 'Grafton' Rail tour which included the Woodford Hulse – Calvert - Verney Junction – Buckingham lines. Here at Verney Junction is Class5 4-6-0 No.45091 heading the train, whilst the RCTS members explore the deserted station. *(6 bells Junction))*

During the above visit this picture was taken of the original sign showing that the station was shared between the Met and the LNWR. However, the Met reference was painted-over in July 1936, when LT withdrew passenger services beyond Quainton Road. The lines to Verney Junction were singled in 1940, but during the war, some specials and trains for local factory workers were run. The tracks were finally removed in 1961. *(6 bells Junction)*

In the foreground are the water cress beds near Waterside on the Chesham branch. It is early in the morning as the sun rises over the Chess Valley in June 1960. Meanwhile commuters head for London over the original bridges on the 08.05 'thorough train' of Dreadnought coaches headed by No.76042, a BR 2-6-0 Class 4MT. *(Colour-Rail)*

On 12th September 1960, the view from Punch Bowl Lane Bridge of the last day of steam operation of the Chesham branch. In the background, the electrification work is complete, – with the new bay platform, intended to accommodate the 'shuttle' and provide a more frequent service – which was never implemented! *(CAF Coll.)*

Another photo of the last day of the Chesham steam shuttle. Here the BR Class 2MT 2-6-2T No.41284 simmers with its three Ashbury coaches in the bay platform at Chalfont & Latimer station. In its usual grimy appearance it carries the traditional laurel wreath on the smokebox door. In the background the goods yard is still in use. *(CAF Coll.)*

The view of the other end of the shuttle at Chalfont & Latimer of the many times modified Ashbury coaches. When the driver was at this end he could control the train by means of links to the regulator and brakes. It is said that one driver used to scare onlookers by ducking down so that he could not be seen! *(CAF Coll.)*

To mark the last day of the Chesham steam shuttle service, LT arranged that the final train of the day would be hauled by the E Class engine No. L44 (Met1). This shows the train in the new bay platform with Dr Arnold Baines, the Chesham Town Mayor, in the cab with the Driver and Fireman. Subsequently, Dr Baines strongly opposed the various attempts by LT to close the branch. *(Dr A. Baines)*

Due to the delays in delivery of the new electric A60 stock, the Chesham shuttle (and some mainline) services initially were operated by T stock trains and Bo-Bo locomotives on the 'through' trains. This shows a three-car 1932 T stock in the bay at Chalfont & Latimer station. *(CAF Coll.)*

LIVE PIGEONS for Liberation

To the Station Master at

STAMPS

PLEASE RELEASE (weather permitting) clear of wires or obstructions. If weather is wet or foggy please return birds unliberated.

Released at

RETURN EMPTY

Time

To ....

STAMPS

Initials

.... STATION.

With the coming of the railways, homing pigeon fanciers were able to practice racing more easily over longer distances by arranging for trains to take their pigeons away and then having them all released at a pre-determined time. *(CAF Coll.)*

In Chesham, the local pigeon fanciers used to meet at the 'Golden Ball' public house and then take their birds to the nearby Met station in baskets. Here in 1960, at Chesham station the empty baskets after 'liberation' are being returned via the T stock shuttle. *(CAF Coll.)*

When the ex-GCR route passed to the Midland Region, they steadily cut services in order to reduce competition with their own from St. Pancras. However, during the rebuilding of Euston station, a number of their trains had to be diverted into Marylebone. Here in 1962, a BR class Britannia No. 70054 'Dornock Moor' is on an up train, having just passed Chorleywood. *(S. Gradidge)*

There were delays in the delivery of the new aluminium A60 stock and limited services began on 12th June 1961. Here one of the first, in pristine condition, is entering Chorleywood station with an 8-car set. These comprised 8-car sets which could be operated as 4-car sets for the Chesham 'shuttle' or used for 'off-peak' traffic. *(S. Gradidge)*

On the 1st October 1961 the Southern Counties Touring Society organised a journey from Stanmore behind E Class L44 via Aldgate East to New Cross Gate. The return was hauled by Bo-Bo electric No16 *'Oliver Goldsmith'*, seen here at Surry Docks station. This was to be its final task before returning to Neasden and being scrapped. *(CAF Coll.)*

With the run-down of services on the ex-GCR line, it was increasingly used for diversions and trials. One of these was of GT3, the gas turbine locomotive developed privately by English Electric/Vulcan which consisted of the turbine mounted on a Class 5 chassis and a tender for diesel fuel. Bound for Nottingham in 1962, it has just passed Chalfont & Latimer, with the Chesham Branch in the background. Unfortunately the concept was overtaken by the commitment to diesel traction and it was scrapped later in 1962. *(british railways tripod.com)*

As part of the Centenary celebrations of the opening of the Metropolitan Railway in 1963, LT arranged a series of events including the refurbishment of several items of Met stock. The highlight was probably the run-past at Neasden Depot of some vintage trains, like the above with E Class Tank engine No.L44 plus a passenger luggage van and Ashbury coaches. Note the full BR goods yard in the background. (*CAF Coll.*)

By 1960's the ubiquitous Stanier Class 5 4-6-0's of the Midland Region hauled most of the few passenger trains going beyond Aylesbury. But following the Beeching Report, the ex-GCR route was closed on 3/9/1966 and here is the last train (with wreath) from Nottingham Victoria leaving Woodford Hulse bound for Marylebone over the Joint line. (*©BNPS.co.uk*)

The BR Modernisation plan of 1958 ushered in the push to diesel traction to replace steam. With little experience in this field, 174 'pilot' diesels were ordered to a variety of designs, quickly followed by production. Sadly, few of the early designs proved satisfactory. These images show the BTC Crewe/Sulzer Type 2 Bo-Bo diesels. The above is No.25314 at Aylesbury in 1982 *(© M. Cook.)* and below is D5088 near Wendover Dean with a parcels train for Marylebone in 1962. *(S. Gradidge)*

In the 1960's there was still quite an amount of steam hauled traffic at Aylesbury. Initially BR renamed it Aylesbury Town (to avoid confusion with the nearby ex-LMS station) but now it has been changed back again. In the foreground, a generally unloved, Class L1 2-6-4T designed by Thompson in 1945 is manoeuvring at the access road to the engine shed. *(Dewi Williams)*

By the early 1960's the lack of engine maintenance was sadly only too visible and coupled with the push to diesel policy, the morale of crews was understandably low. This is clearly shown by the state of this locomotive shunting at Rickmansworth. No.42252 is a 2-6-4T designed by Fairburn for the LMS in 1945, being a shorter wheelbase version of an earlier Fowler design. *(S. Gradidge)*

Following the Beeching Report recommendations and the negative attitude of BR Midland Region, by Christmas 1965 it was decided to close the GCR London Extension beyond Aylesbury. That winter with a thin covering of snow, 'Black Five' 4-6-0 No.45089 presses on near Pinner bound for Nottingham. *(R. Fisher)*

After Met services were withdrawn to Verney Junction and the tracks singled, the lines at the station were used to store redundant stock. Possibly the strangest occupants were in 1964 when some ex-LMS Euston/ Broad Street EMU's were awaiting scrapping. *(LURS)*

In 1957 a train eventually bound for Aylesbury approaches Rickmansworth station, where the staff will nonchalantly perform their well-practiced routine for the changeover to steam haulage. On the footbridge the schoolboy train spotters watch the Bo-Bo No. 5 *'John Hampden'*, whilst in the siding is the BR tank engine from the previous up train. *(S. Gradidge)*

The 1959 scene at Farringdon station from beside another train for Aylesbury, which is headed by Bo-Bo electric locomotive No.7 *'Edmund Burke'* (both the names of this and the previous photo were notable MP's of Wendover, on the Met). Ahead and to the right was the site of the main Met Goods Depot at Vine Street. *(H. F. Wheeler)*

Extra tracks (known as the 'Widened Lines') were added between Kings Cross and Moorgate to cope with the extra traffic created by the mainline companies adjacent to the Met. Looking west from Farringdon, with a point giving access from the Met in the foreground, is a BR Cravens DMU and an LT C69 stock train travelling in the opposite direction. *(CAF Coll.)*

Looking east from Farringdon station over the Widened Lines, with on the left the Met tracks to the Barbican, in the middle the Met Farringdon sidings and to the right the lines lead to Moorgate. *(Nick Bailey)*

As a consequence of the machinations of Watkin and Forbes, Whitechapel ended up with two stations. The MDR extended their joint line with the Met from St. Mary's Junction (in conjunction with the LTSR) via Whitechapel to Campbell Road Junction. This competed with the existing Met station ('low level') on the ELR, seen above with an A60 stock train. *(Metropolitan Matt)*

For refurbishment the A60 stock were returned to the manufacturer, then Cravens, at Derby. Seen here at Amersham station in 1994, a set of the A60's are being returned to Neasden Depot. They are hauled behind a BR Type 37 diesel locomotive, with a match wagon to accommodate the different couplings. *(Trevor Rolf)*

In the 1950's a number of the Bo-Bo electric locomotives were withdrawn, some continued in service (with improved braking systems), some used for testing various brake blocks and No.1 *(John Lyon)* relegated to shunting duties at Neasden. For this it was fitted with buckeye couplings to deal with the new A60 stock and the disposal of the T stock. *(CAF Coll.)*

Chorleywood is said to be the coldest place on the Met and it certainly seems so in this view in January 1962, where just north of the station, an up train of one of the remaining T stock trains has stalled in the snow. The little warmth in the train is shown around the ventilators and the hanging icicles. *(Chris Gooch/ David Hibbert)*

Looking north at Harrow on the Hill station in 1971. On the right are usually the fast & stopping up platforms, then the down ones and out of sight on the left, those for Marylebone. Both trains are of the A60 stock, which were one of the last LT multiple-electric trains to have separate motoring and braking controls. They were subsequently to have major refurbishments at Adtranz/Bombardier in 1993 to 1998 when the Guards positions were removed and car-end windows fitted. *(CAF Coll.)*

The 'last' steam hauled Met train ran on the 6th June 1971, seen here at Barbican station hauled by ex-GWR (7752) 0-6-0 pannier tank now L94, with a variety of LT service stock. *(CAF Coll.)*

Inspired by the celebratory special trains marking the Centenary of the Met reaching Chesham, a series of 'Steam on the Met' events were held for several years, featuring a number of preserved locomotives, such as the above Gresley Class B12 4-6-0 No.61572, approaching Chorleywood in the year 2000. Although these ceased for 'health & safety' reasons, special events have continued with *'Sarah Siddons'* and Met 1. (*RCTS*)

Over the years many unusual events, apart from those caused by extreme weather conditions, have disrupted the Chesham Branch line. More recent incidents include - a bicycle dropped on the tracks creating a short circuit, a runaway van blocking the line, a swan alighting on the track and the above tree blown over in high winds. (*CAF Coll.*)

Bombardier was given the contract to produce the replacement for all the LUL sub-surface stock. A southbound S8 variant (of 8 cars) is seen between Preston Road and Wembley Park on the 'local' line at Stanmore Junction on 2 March 2015, passing over the flyunder for the Stanmore line which was provided from November 1938, hitherto it being a flat junction – also see p75. *(Brian Hardy)*

The Chesham Shuttle was soon replaced by through services of A60 and then the new S8 stock and this shows the arrival of the last A60 stock shuttle train into the dedicated bay at Chalfont and Latimer station, on the night of the 11th December 2010. *(rmweb)*

Watkin would be pleased! His schemes to reach Oxford and spite the GWR never came to pass, but now Chiltern Railways have built at Bicester a chord (shown above) from their mainline to Birmingham, joining the ex-LNWR line between Oxford and Cambridge. This will give them a direct service to Oxford. Indirectly it also forms part of the planed renewal of the important East–West link which might see the-reopening of Verney Junction. *(Phil Marsh/RM)*

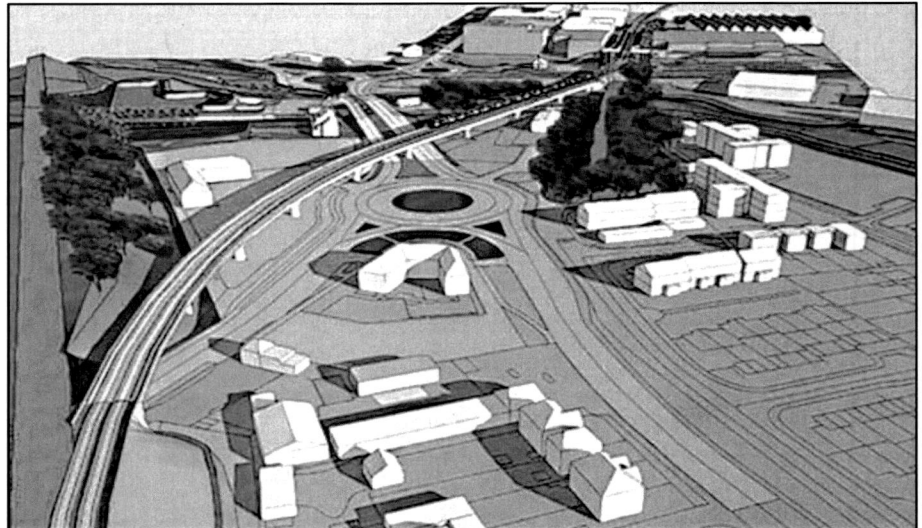

The creation of British Railways initiated a proposal to join the Met branch to Watford with that of the LMS Croxley branch in order to give access to Watford Town Centre and the Junction. This received much support, but by the year 2000 costs had risen to £48M and now stand at £250M. Above is the proposed link, with on the left, the original Met tracks to Watford station and on the top right the Croxley branch.